OFF-ROAD HARRY

Tracey Hawkins
Dillon Naylor

RISING ★ STARS

For my parents, for worrying about my escapades
For Simon, for sharing them

First published in the UK by
Rising Stars UK Ltd.
7 Hatchers Mews, Bermondsey Street, London SE1 3GS
www.risingstars-uk.com

This edition published 2011

Text © UC Publishing Pty Ltd.
www.ucpublishing.com

First published 2006 by Insight Publications Pty Ltd.
ABN 57 005 102 983,
89 Wellington Street,
St Kilda, Victoria 3182
Australia

Development: UC Publishing Pty Ltd
Cover design: UC Publishing/Design Ed
Written by: Tracey Hawkins
Illustrations: Dillon Naylor
Text design and typesetting: Design Ed/Clive Sutherland
Editorial consultancy: Dee Reid

All rights reserved. No part of this publication may be reproduced, stored in a retrieval system or transmitted in any form by any means, electronic, mechanical, photocopying, recording or otherwise without the prior permission of Rising Stars Ltd.

British Library Cataloguing in Publication Data.
A CIP record for this book is available from the British Library.

ISBN: 978-1-84680-811-1

Printed by Craft Print International Ltd., Singapore

Contents

Chapter 1 An off-road adventure 5

Chapter 2 Gearing up 8

Chapter 3 The training track 11

Chapter 4 Making tracks 16

Chapter 5 Out of control 20

Chapter 6 A major collision 26

Chapter 7 'You can do it' 31

Chapter 8 Back to the base 34

Chapter 9 Back on the track 37

North Tyneside Libraries	
LBN	
3 8012 01788 2292	
Askews & Holts	27-Jun-2011
J H	£4.99

Chapter 1
An off-road adventure

Harry followed his dad up the busy street. He was in Queenstown, New Zealand— the 'Adventure Capital of the World'. All around him were shops selling fantastic tours and adventures. Everything from bungy jumping and skydiving to white-water rafting and jet-boating.

But Harry didn't want to do any of it. He had said 'No' to everything his father had suggested. It wasn't that he was a coward. He just liked to be careful. He didn't want to get hurt again.

Harry used to love going as fast as he possibly could. Skateboarding, bike riding— the faster, the better. Then one day a car had knocked him from his bike. Harry's leg was broken in two places. It had taken him months to recover. Sometimes his leg still ached.

'Look at this, Harry,' said his father, Dr Edwards. He pointed at a display of four-wheeled bikes outside a shop called Off-Road Tours. 'Isn't that an amazing motorbike?'

'Yeah, it's cool,' said Harry, hoping he sounded excited.

'It's a kid's quad bike,' said a voice beside them. 'They're for off-road adventures.'

'What's an off-road adventure?' asked Harry.

'It's a load of fun,' said the man. 'You can ride a quad bike just about anywhere—in the dirt, up mountains and, best of all, through mud.'

Dr Edwards looked at Harry. 'Fancy an off-road adventure, son?'

'Well … I'm not sure,' said Harry. 'I've never done anything like this before.'

'That's OK,' said the salesman. 'We can teach you to ride one. We've got something to suit everyone. Why don't you come inside and watch our video? It will show you what we do.'

Chapter 2
Gearing up

Harry peered through the window of the Off-Road Tours minibus. It was freezing outside and snow showers were expected later in the day.

He looked over at the two boys sitting across from him. Jack and Dan were 17-year-old twin brothers. They were laughing, cracking jokes and calling out to the driver. Harry guessed they weren't feeling anxious like he was.

The driver pointed to a towering mountain just ahead. 'That's where we're going,' he said. He turned off the highway, drove along a dirt track and pulled up beside a big metal shed.

In front of the shed were some quad bikes. A young man, wearing an orange waterproof suit, was waiting outside the shed. An older woman with a walking stick was standing next to him.

Harry, his father and the twins jumped down from the bus. The young man came up to them.

'Hi, I'm Mark,' he said. 'I'll be leading the tour today. This is my grandmother, Mrs Turner. Come in and we'll get the gear you'll need.'

When everyone was ready, Mark led them to the bikes. Four large quad bikes were lined up together. Off to one side was a smaller, yellow quad bike.

'This one is for you,' Mark told Harry. 'It's a 50cc Suzuki. It's got plenty of power for someone your age.'

Dan and Jack laughed. 'It looks like a yellow smartie on wheels,' teased Dan.

Harry felt foolish. He ignored the twins and climbed on the quad. It felt safe. Maybe a ride wouldn't be too bad.

Chapter 3
The training track

Mark showed them how to start their quad bikes and use the throttle lever to control the quad's speed. Harry pushed the lever, getting a feel for how it responded to the flick of his thumb. He looked over at the others. He hoped he could keep up with them.

Soon the group was ready to start riding.

'OK, start your engines,' yelled Mark.

Harry turned on his ignition switch and slowly released the brake. The bike jerked forward. He grabbed the brake handle. His bike shuddered to a stop and Harry almost fell off. His heart began to pound.

'Take it slow and steady,' said Mark. 'Apply the brake with a softer touch. You'll be fine.'

Harry took a deep breath and started up his bike again. This time, he eased off the brake and the quad moved forward.

Mark went first and the others fell into a line behind him. They drove around the small training track. The track was a dirt road with small dips and rises. It would help the riders get used to their quads.

Harry found he could manage his bike quite well. It didn't have any gears like the bigger bikes, just the throttle and brake.

They came to a deep dip. Bundy showed them how to steer the bike through the ruts and up the other side. Harry and his father tried hard and moved through the dip without any problems.

Jack and Dan hadn't been listening to Mark. They both almost rolled their quads sideways when they hit a huge rut.

'Hey, you two,' yelled Mark, 'be careful. Do as I tell you, or you might get hurt.'

Chapter 4
Making tracks

'One more loop and we'll be ready to go out on the tracks,' Mark told the group.

'How are you doing?' Dr Edwards called to Harry.

'Great. This is awesome,' Harry yelled back. He was quite surprised to find that he meant it. He had enjoyed the training track.

Mark led them through the gate and along a dirt track. Once out in the open, he picked up the pace. Harry flicked his throttle forward, increasing his speed to keep up. He was feeling anxious, but he still felt a smile creep across his face.

The group followed Mark to the base of a hill, where he stopped. 'We're going up,' he said, pointing to the small hill. 'Give it lots of throttle to get up and then ease off at the top.'

One by one, the riders went up the hill and disappeared over the top. Harry leaned forward and gently pushed the throttle lever. He clung to the handlebars as the quad crawled up the slope.

Going down the other side was trickier. Harry felt as if he was going to slide off the front of the bike. He rammed his feet on the footpads and sat up straight. He hit a few big bumps but managed to control the quad.

But on the last big bump, things went wrong. The quad bike rose up into the air, then came crashing down. Harry's feet flew sideways. He grabbed the handlebars but he lost control of his bike and shot off into the scrub.

Harry let go of the throttle and took two deep breaths to calm down. 'OK, I'm fine,' he told himself. 'I survived.' He forced himself to start riding again. A few minutes later, he was roaring along the track to catch up to the group.

The others were waiting at the edge of the clearing. Harry soon saw why. There in front of him was the biggest, muddy puddle he had ever seen.

Chapter 5
Out of control

'This is the bit where you get dirty,' grinned Mark.

He explained how to ride the bike through the mud. 'Don't put your feet down—you could get hurt,' he said.

One at a time, the group pushed through the mud. They went slipping and sliding as the wheels squelched through the mud.

Harry zoomed off. His bike slid sideways. Mud splattered across his suit. He tried to straighten up. His knuckles turned white from gripping the handlebar. The wheels skidded one way, then another.

Then, the bike hit a deep rut. Both Harry and his quad flew up in the air. 'Aarrgghh!' he screamed. The quad landed with a bang and skidded into the muddy bog.

Harry held on tightly. He pulled hard on the handlebar, and the bike slid to one side. Somehow, he managed to straighten up in time to see what lay ahead.

'Oh no!' thought Harry. He plunged into the deepest part of the puddle.

Mud sprayed out the sides of the wheels like a waterfall. The bike slid across the wet, oozy mud. Harry squeezed on the brake, held his breath and came to a shuddering halt just near the group.

'Look at you,' laughed Dr Edwards. 'Wasn't that great?'

'Yeah, great,' gasped Harry. He couldn't believe he'd managed to get through the mud without crashing.

Mark came up and patted him on the back. 'Wow, Harry. Cool driving. But next time, if

you want to slow down, take your thumb off the throttle.

Throttle? Harry felt like a real idiot when he realised what he'd done. He had been so busy hanging on, he'd somehow pushed the throttle forwards instead of backwards.

Chapter 6
A major collision

They rode for another hour, until it was time to head back. Mark warned them about the need to stay in his track.

'Going down a mountain can be more dangerous than going up,' he said. 'This is the steepest part of the mountain. Just do as I say and you'll be fine. Harry, you follow behind me.'

Harry moved his quad behind Mark.

Mark turned back to him. 'Sit back in your seat, thumb off the throttle. Don't put your foot down when we hit the mud. Watch me,' he said and headed off.

Harry started down the steep slope. The quad's wheels bounced over the rocks and bumps and into the mud. He steered the quad into Mark's tracks. The front wheels slipped

and the bike slid sideways. Harry felt it tip but he straightened up. He eased out of the mud and came to the bottom of the hill.

'Great stuff!' yelled Mark as Harry pulled up beside him.

Harry couldn't stop grinning. His heart thumped in his chest and his hands felt clammy but he hadn't felt this good in ages.

Last to ride down the slope were Jack and Dan. 'Last one down is a loser!' yelled Dan. He roared off, with Jack hot on his tail.

'They're going too fast and they're too close together,' cried Mark. 'Slow down!' he yelled, but they couldn't hear him above the noise of the engines.

Harry held his breath as he watched the twins zigzag down the mountain. Jack got too close behind Dan. Dan skidded into the mud at full speed. He lost control and the bike shot sideways.

Jack couldn't avoid him. He smashed into Dan's quad, sending Dan flying. Jack flew down the last few metres and smashed into Mark, waiting at the bottom.

Chapter 7
'You can do it'

The next few minutes were a blur for Harry. He sat frozen as memories of his own accident came flooding back.

As if watching a movie, he saw Dan crawling over to his brother. Jack lay on his back, not far from his quad. Harry heard him groaning in pain. He could see Mark lying trapped under his bike.

'Harry, help me,' called Dr Edwards. Harry heard his father but couldn't seem to move. 'Harry! I need you now!' Harry slid off his bike and went to help.

Mark was conscious but his ankle was bent at a funny angle.

'My backpack,' Mark whispered. 'First aid kit. Call base for help.'

Dr Edwards found a small medical kit and a walkie talkie in Mark's backpack.

'Harry, call the base for help,' he said. 'I need to see to Dan and Jack.' He moved over to the twins. 'Don't worry,' he said. 'I'm a doctor. I'll look after you.'

Harry flicked the on switch and called into the walkie talkie. But all he could hear was static. 'It's not working,' he cried.

'The signal must be blocked by the mountains,' said Dr Edwards. 'Harry, Jack's got a few cracked ribs, Dan is concussed and Mark has a broken ankle. I need you to go back to the office and get help.'

Go back alone! Harry felt a rise of panic. 'Dad, I don't think I can. I'm not a good enough rider.'

'Harry, listen to me. I know you're scared,' Dad's voice was firm, 'but you can do it— I know you can. I'm needed here. You must go for help.'

Harry knew he had to go. He had to get over his fear. 'OK,' he said. 'I'll go.'

He started up the quad and turned back to the trail. He'd never felt so scared in his life.

Chapter 8
Back to the base

By the time Harry got near the base, the sky was getting dark. 'OK, Harry. You *can* do this,' he muttered.

He reached the muddy bog and slowed. He used just enough throttle to keep moving. He got through the mud and shot through the long grass. He rode as fast as he dared and made it back to the clearing. He kept saying to himself, 'Don't panic, you can do this.'

A flurry of snowflakes caught him by surprise. It made it harder to see. He stopped the quad and looked ahead. How much further could it be?

After what seemed like forever, Harry reached the metal shed.

'Help! Help! I need help,' yelled Harry as he pulled up beside the office.

Mrs Turner hobbled out as fast as she could. When she saw Harry, she stopped in her tracks. Harry was a sight—covered in mud from head to toe—and alone.

'There's been an accident,' Harry gasped. 'Mark and the twins are hurt. Dad is looking after them until we can get help to them.'

Mrs Turner phoned at once for an ambulance.

'They're on their way,' she told Harry. 'I can't believe you came all that way by yourself. It must have been hard in the snow—you've been very brave.' She hugged the tired boy. 'But if this weather gets worse, the ambulance won't be able to get through. We'll have to take two trailers back and bring Mark and the boys to a pick-up point.'

'Go back—and towing a trailer?' thought Harry. How could he manage to do it all again? How was old Mrs Turner going to manage?

'Can you ride a quad?' asked Harry.

She gave him a smile. 'I've been riding motorbikes since I was a girl. I grew up on a farm. Now, I'll get some supplies, then we'll get the quads ready to go back.'

Chapter 9
Back on the track

Mrs Turner fixed trailers to two quads. She packed a medical kit, blankets and other supplies into the trailers.

Harry helped her pack his trailer. He wasn't sure about towing anything, but he knew he didn't have a choice.

'Right, we're ready,' said Mrs Turner. She sat on the big quad, revved it up and roared off towards the gate.

Harry almost laughed in surprise. Mrs Turner was a rev head!

Not wanting to be left behind, Harry jumped on his quad. He could feel the extra weight of the trailer as the bike roared forward.

The falling snow grew thicker. The wind whipped the snow across Harry's helmet, making it very hard to see. All of a sudden, Harry realised there was a dark shape in front of him. He jammed on the brakes.

Mrs Turner leaned over Harry's quad. 'You'll need to stick close to me. I don't want to lose you. It's getting much harder to see.'

Harry nodded. He didn't fancy getting lost in the storm. He'd never find his way in a blizzard.

'You're very brave, Harry,' said Mrs Turner. 'Not many kids could have done what you did.'

Harry was amazed. He didn't think he was brave. In fact, he had been terrified the whole trip back. But he'd known that the others were counting on him.

'At least I got help,' he thought. 'Now, we just need to find the others before the storm gets worse.'

Harry released his brake and followed Mrs Turner up the mountains. The next part of his adventure was just beginning …